Vacating the Premises

Vacating the Premises

by

Page Nelson

Another Sparrow
Press

ISBN: 978-1-941066-15-7
Cataloging-at-Publication data
Nelson, Page, 1952-
Vacating the premises /by Page Nelson.
    1. Aphorisms and apothegms.
    II. Title.   2017. RDA-NEG8
PN6271.N4433 2017   CAP/NOTCIP

Catalogued to pre-2014 conventions in conformity with standards approved by the American Association of Cataloging Rules Conservation (AACRC).

Book design by Jo-Anne Rosen.
Author's portrait by Publius Porcius Portraiture and Photography.

The author has quoted and adapted one passage of Schopenhauer's "On Style" from the translation by T. Bailey Saunders in *The Pessimist's Handbook*.

All illustrations are by the author, reproduced in black and white (excepting the covers) from the oil on canvas (5"x 5") originals. For a price-list and additional information, contact Guy Mantis Galleries, New York.

Vacate:

1. To leave empty or unoccupied.
2. To cancel, annul or void a judgment.

Premises:

1. Foundational or primary propositions.
2. A building, house or place of habitation.

Preface

Vacating the Premises is the last and least of my experiments in aphoristic exposition. The book's three parts – dicta, personal positions and micro-essays, vary in their configurations of truthful intent and content. Topically, aesthetics, contemporary poetry, love, treachery and death are addressed in a typically practical and cheerful manner. Paintings (reduced to black and white) from my already existing body of amateurish art were selected as illustrations when I detected a thematic resonance between image and proposition. Should even one reader, advised to read sporadically and *in particular*, find any item of interest (this collection lacking any intention to please), the author's hopes for the book will have been fulfilled. I am indebted to Rosaline Felis for moral support through the duration of the project. Of course, I am solely responsible for all content and any eros.

Dicta

"I fancy mankind may come in time to write all aphoristically, grown weary of all those arts by which a big book is made." Dr Johnson, quoted in Boswell's *Journal of a Tour of the Hebrides.*[1]

Aphorists are anti-systematic; that is their system.[2]

Dicta are the quanta of literary meaning; being minute, the force of focus alters them.

The strange life process where to become one's self, one must become "not others".

Perfect hell: the place where you feel the pain you have inflicted on others only without this knowledge so that you are denied the consolation of justice.

Everything needs a limit to have value. Even those apparent absolutes, love and beauty, are marginally sustained by ugliness and indifference.

I can't know the sun will rise tomorrow but I believe it. I know I will die but I don't believe it. These are the surveying poles of human knowledge.

Two principles of bibliographic physics: many books, interesting to write, are boring to read; no book interesting to read was boring to write.

Most art that matters is dressing to a wound.[3]

The most extraordinary thing is the most familiar thing – our perception of time and space, our just walking down a road or sitting in a chair. There is more wisdom in retaining this sense of strangeness than in whole folios of mystical lore or decades of guruic instruction.[4]

Between most couples lies a body of betrayal and that's the body they make love to.

Get up early. Nothing is more exciting than seeing the sun rise on a new day of work and rest, beauty and shame, pleasure and pain.

To be approved for one's vices and disparaged for one's virtues, that was the workplace – sometimes, not always; another thing not to be relied on.

How often one has wished for oblivion – but only on one's own terms.

We relate to guilt like – a hackneyed phrase that's apt – water off a duck's back. See it shimmy and give a flick of its beak. Likewise life-floaters, we need to maintain a buoyant good opinion of ourselves.

Contrary to the cliché. The guilty sleep easily. It is their victims who toss and turn.

The Buddhists are, no doubt, right about the virtues of Emptiness but keep in mind it's not called emptiness for nothing.

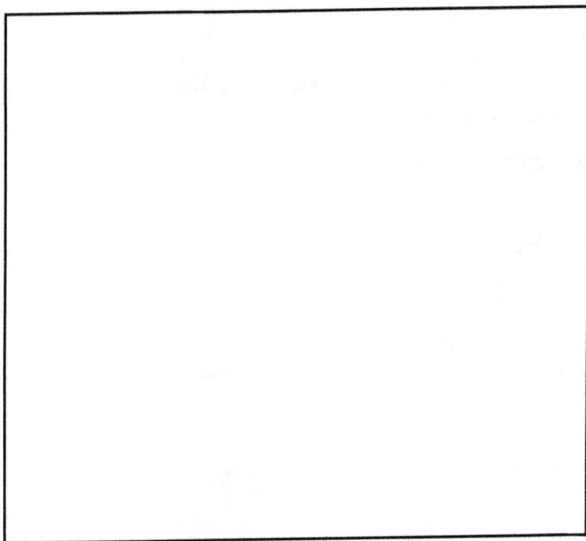

The failure of love, of the many hells exclusively reserved for the living, is one of the loneliest and most instantaneous.

The garden must die that the garden might live. A better ground for philosophy than most.

We demonstrate our fundamental hopefulness in thinking we can get away with crime. (And generally we do, provided the crimes aren't merely legal ones.)

Funny how most wisdom is past its sell-by date which is to say, its self-buy date.

The miracles are light, life and love, in that generative order.

Understanding our capacity for unhappiness is almost a comfort in the way certain aches are almost pleasures. (We acquire knowledge of our limit and it is larger than we supposed.)

Beware the extreme beauty; having been incessantly assaulted by admiration and sexual tendering, he or she is primed for retaliation.

Few things are more visually addictive than a cat.

The only American art objects destined to endure for five hundred years, a basic metric for classics, are the manhole covers underfoot, those iron mandalas resistant to facile burnishing (praise) and to that most persistent critic, decay.

Sand mandala. Make distinctions, then blur them. (But don't suppose the second action is superior to the first.)

The lacey waves lapped his feet, the sun warmed, the breeze cooled his skin, sea birds laughed … with the next step, he was in over his head and struggling. *Moral: it is naive to think you can test the waters and not be tested by them.*

Self pity; self poisoning.

These glints, swept up from my stream of thought, may be pyrite or gold but in either case, they have been swirled about, appraised, picked out, panned you might say or more precisely, pained.

He was one of those self-contained types; his heart could only be opened by breaking.

Human love has been expressed and explicated to the point of tedium. My cat's affections are as yet miraculous and mysterious.

Our lives occur not on a plain but on a terrain of complex contours where, for example, you are naturally biased to have more friends than enemies, where no enemies will become real friends but where true friends will become deep enemies – these just three of the many intersecting inclinations.

Clinically, one is often asked to evaluate and report one's physical pain on a scale of one to ten. For mental pain, put this diagnostic question – is the pain in the present tense? ("yes" = "ten").

The Buddhists are right; we are seduced into rebirth by sex. Those that had good sex want more and those who never did want some.

The benediction of rain.

After you have paced your mind's length, breadth and depth, it's time not to settle in but to vacate the premises.

Forgiveness is something you do for yourself. Revenge, something you do to others, is to that extent generous and who would separate generosity from charity?

Her face was the perfect expression of the purpose of beauty in nature: attraction, deception.

An elation of liars.

Nothing is more life-enhancing than a talent for forgetting.

The stadium was impressive – a state of the art facility for wasting one's life in.

High wind in trees: a deep lesson about force, resisting it and yielding.

Rock music=ego amplification; the genre became and has stayed popular because that is what people want to hear. In McLuhanian terms, the multi-decibeled medium is the message.

Late news from Elsinore. What a shame that our Hamlet, needing a wholesome hobby, chose fencing.

A person you assume you don't want to spend time with – a stranger. A person you know you don't – a friend.

The decisions we made and the ones that were made for us — we were content and went deeper into the labyrinth.[5]

Since no animal is intentionally cruel or self-debasing, we are wrong to use "bestial" as a condemnatory term. For Amon Goeth, for King Leopold's Congo managers, for any serial killer you'd care to name, there's another word right at hand. Humane.

Art is overrated, art is underrated. Art, properly, is thus equivocated.[6]

Too much art kills culture, too much information kills knowledge, too much connectivity kills relation, too much choice kills freedom, too many renderings of reality obliterate reality.[7]

Capital punishment makes one queasy, from fellow feeling and at the possibility of a mistake. But when in every land, the innocent poor expire from not having food, shelter and medical care as good as the state's prisoners, why should proven murderers be sustained?

The co-incidence, that the human mind can access mathematics to model the universe is so extraordinary it requires an explanation other than co-incidence.

In mid-life, it "dawned" on him that his way of life was a way of death. But so was everybody else's.[8]

We are wiser than we know – and more foolish. Our lives take place in a state of duplex ignorance.[9]

It's a safe assumption that we are entirely material beings. But what is matter?

Personal Positions

At age sixty, I'd worked through the thicket of sex –
with scars to prove it*. I saw ahead of me such vistas of
possibilities, why in just a decade or two of undistracted
development, I'd become the person I'd always wanted
to be. (*The scars sealing not only wounds, but mouths
that pleasured.)

I started calling our pet the names I could no longer use
on you, *darling, sweetheart, my dear.* That would teach
you. It did. Soon you were doing the same thing. The
cat was much loved.

My most precious living possession – my enemy. In
him I invested absolute trust, confident he would never
betray me with beguilements of friendship. (Or, as the
case might be, never again.)

The point of my life? – this focus, here and now.

I planted the new tree in the ground, thinking it will survive me. It was nothing profound.

After my friend injured me, seeing him flee from me in the library stacks or his doing a 180-degree retreat down the street, I'd laugh out loud, an outburst of belated victory. You see, he had told me that if anyone ever violated him in the way he had me, he'd shoot them. It was almost if not quite the funniest thing I ever experienced – to think that after what had happened, he thought I'd follow his example in anything, including his punishment.

My friend said he liked my "bon mutts" –as he pronounced it. It's true they are loyal and lie around me like dogs.

Like alcohol or drugs in their good phase, I get too much pleasure from my Ego (sense of self) to give it up. The sages say Ego is "always-already" poisonous but I doubt it. Indeed, the Ego merits a more intensive curation, giving us as it does, via its focal points of pleasure and pain, our sharp vision of the world.

It is perhaps not too shameful to record: I had acquired a taste, a longing for catastrophe but when it came I was satisfied with just a taste.

Beyond the shadow line, that meridian of just declining maturity, is the twilight line. Crossing it, I live for dreams, my dream life being so much more varied, forceful and vivacious than daily life which seems the poorest kind of dream, beginning always in a muddled middle that's tediously repetitive and goes, is going, on too long.

In adolescence, self-consciously aware of being "normal" or at least unexceptional, I aspired to become to be a complex-interesting person, a character out of Henry James. Now after endless negotiations with the irremediable, I'd happily choose to be average, boring, and conventionally confident. Alas, the success of my originating ambition has spoiled those options forever.

It never occurred to me that the day would come (and all the days thereafter) when I would curse that I'd been honest, that a special Boschean hell is reserved for truth tellers. There *was* the usual consolation: since I hadn't foreseen it, I'd gotten exactly what I deserved.

I was not naturally an aphorist since my tendency was always to wonder – why use one word when two or three will do?

Your enemies haven't the slightest consideration for your well-being. Surely, the highest possible compliment of your strength.

I know I will die but I do not believe it. I believe my work is meritorious but I do not know it. At this most import intersection of the belief's longitude and knowledge's latitude, I have no fixture; location 0.00, 0.00.

The real cheat. Within weeks, you ceased being tensile steel and became porcelain. Still beautiful, you were suddenly fragile, strangely vulnerable so that I could not now (new complaint), subject you to the force of my old one.

He felt like a king in a losing end-game, no good squares left.

Try I might, I can't overcome my feeling that the sexually unfaithful are disgusting (the stain being the deceit, not the sex), that such betrayers merit death but … don't deserve to die. One is placed in a morally awkward position and disposed not to thank the positioners even if they have endowed one with a superior sense of life's ambiguities. For instance, treachery is always willed and cruel, while betrayal is something one might just stumble upon. Or so they say.

Like most people imposed upon (I hesitate to say "wronged",) my initial and longest response was "why me?" which has all the utility of trying to sail into a head wind. Gradually I tacked around to a position of "why *not* me?" If not a true course, it allowed forward motion.

"The light thronged glass" or "light thronging the glass" who wrote that? Larkin, I think. I wish I had. I wrote "light by the glass's flaw captivate", not quite the same idea and not half as good. But wasn't he a constipated old sexist-racist with three abject mistresses?

Mary, who worked in his department and whom he knew by name and sometimes said hello to, came up to him at the party and said "Susan (whom he knew only as Mary's friend, also at the party) thinks you look okay but have ghastly mannerisms." He was dumbfounded. What were *mannerisms* and which of his (all?) were ugly? Why would Mary say such a thing? Had Susan asked her to? Was it some kind of weird "come-on", from her, from Mary? Was it aggression – on Susan's part or Mary's or both because he had never come-on to them? It was one of those embarrassing things you remember your entire life (when you have forgotten many more important matters) and shameful because you've retained it. And only to be written about in the third person.

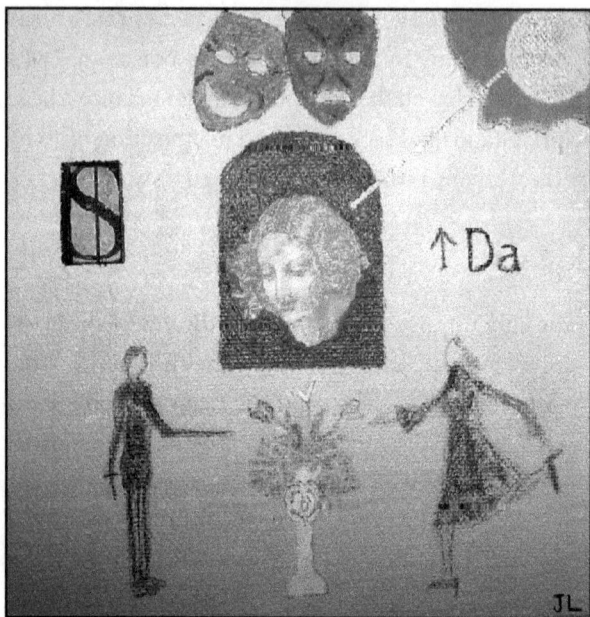

It was my friends (who else) who passed to me the cup of treachery and bade me drink, drink deep down to the spider. Among the toxic effects was a strange illumination, I could for the first time feel (rather than observe) the actuality of good and evil. My own injurious actions were no longer ignorable; I bore them as elements of a new gravity. I was on the earth in a way I had never been. So, should I be grateful to these friends or should I put a bullet through their heads? My daily mediation.

The only reader that interested him – the rarest kind, lex-ically saturated and over refined, who having ceased read-ing from fatigue, would in former times have refreshed himself by the intensities of poetry except now poetry was so debased it impeached even the classics. In other words, a typical kind of author, he wrote for himself.

Increasingly, the four or five beings I have most loved (including cats) and the two subjects I most revered (Schumann and Shakespeare) diminish like ports viewed backwards from a new dimension, vast and featureless.

After a period of exciting exploration, there were years of friendship, followed by decades of involvement that had positive aspects of a partnership and negative ones of a taking for granted – in other words a marriage, in this case to alcohol and not a bad one. If it had shaved a few years off his life, he suspected it also had added a few. It had all worked out. And he was never alone.

It was the confluence of a big thing (relative to one human life) – decades of reading and experience, and a small one – a modest writing ability seldom exercised, never developed and just on the point of expiration, that made the strictly temporary micro clime where these dicta, fall flowers, might germinate.

A certain slant of light. Angst and longing, common afflictions of adolescence, are variably manifested in individuals. I felt there were ecstasies in being hurt and that the most definitive meaning lodged in defeat. The only "objective correlative" for this feeling was the intense azure of late autumn and early winter twilights, augmented later by my discovery of certain lines by Dickenson and Schumann's contrapuntal turnings. I couldn't wait to leave home and find my fate, not knowing it finds you and in ways you could never conceive.

One's position was passive but there was still satisfaction in setting forth. It seemed a free action and the essential pre-condition for whatever followed.

I was happy 90% of my life and lest this make me instantly dismissible if not despicable (no one wishes to hear of others' contentment) let me hasten to add I was never happy about my happiness. I was always waiting for some hammer to fall or felt as if I were remiss to leave the sad oboe and melancholy viola sitting on their chairs unplayed, a one person orchestra who didn't know the score.

In the object of my affections, I chose passion over fidelity, beauty over truth and if I wasn't happy in the circumstances of the choice, I was gratified to have had the chance of making it – and for the starkness of the terms.

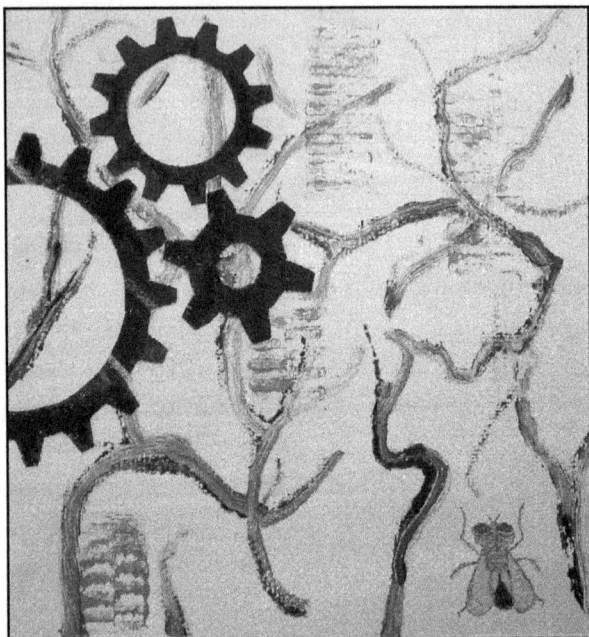

My resistance to the inexorable was, I guess, part of it.

Definitely a Robert Shallow type: anxious, eccentrically semi -narcissistic, "humorous", dutiful (along certain limited lines), superficially deferential but always looking out for "the main chance" (if unsure exactly what that might be). If he couldn't gratifyingly boast of *bona robas* and hearing the chimes at midnight, he had seen the fireflies rise, many times. It was enough.

My life seemed a void. However much I threw into it, lovers, habits, hobbies, eating and drinking, walks, TV, reading, (so much reading!) . . . it stayed empty, it always wanted more. But this was wrong. It's more like a pipe or conduit. A pipe, in use, is never empty or full. It's a matter of flows, rates of flows. Now I had a new motto. *Go with the flow.*

I would no more organize these dicta topically than I would plant a garden in ranks of roses, zones of zinnias, plots of pansies. My flowers follow from the free fall of seed.

With this exception. Not being a morbid person, it seems discourteous to leave my thoughts on death just scattered about where any reader might stumble upon them at random, an enactment of the event itself. But it must be allowed that the longer one lives, death becomes more and more an object of practical and speculative interest as "the next big thing." Shakespeare himself, through that magnanimous megaphone, Prospero, says that in retirement his every third thought will be about death. Mine (only a fourth of this section) are grouped below and continue for one page, to be read if one is in the mood or, more happily, skipped.

At the exhibition opening: several hundred prosperous, older people and me – wondering why death has not yet undone them. Yet the individual consciousness at seventy may be more spry and open minded than one at twenty and all think themselves in that category, all value their lives. Certainly there is reason for compassion seeing the fate portended in these old bodies. Yet what a sense of irritation at so many being in the habit of living, in their predictable mechanics of good digestion and conversation. In a crowded world, why are these people, myself included, even here?

I think expiring in the act of love would be the ideal death except for the horror it imposes on one's partner. We need to devise and perfect techniques of autoerotic thanatos, death by wanking, the Western Bardo Thodol, though at the rate we're going, erotic robots, the ultimate technical solution, are just around the corner.

I used to get up every day with the thought, "this could be my last day", a life enhancing mediation. Now it just annoys me, like waiting for an overdue package or having missed an appointment.

I like doctors but doctors in their need to know can kill you. Finally, there's the beyond dispute answer – you're dead.

My doctor said my chronic medical condition meant I had a 10% chance of dying each year over the next decade. Don't feel bad, it's not so bad he said, at your age the rate is 5-6% anyway. We laughed. What could be better, a jocular doctor. But at the end of ten years what? I've made such a contribution to the world: nine published poems, three adopted cats, two loved wives, the email protocol at the community college, etc., etc. I have so much more to do. There must be some mistake.

Death is frequently described as a "friend" or enemy. I think of it as the hard-shouldered stranger who runs into you as you rush about your business and knocks you breathless without a word of apology either way.

However much I attempt it, I cannot get my mind around death. There is some psychological, biological conceptual barrier. Living, we cannot understand "not-life", a natural prohibition perhaps lest we should come to desire it. Or put another way, the fear of death makes us value life; the knowledge of death might have another effect entirely.

He needed to have lived a long time before he could understand the truthful force of the cliché "life is short." But he also thought "Short compared to what?" (You need time to live, love and work but once you have done those things, to say "life is short" amounts to a complaint that your life will ever end, which means you could live a million years and still find life too short. This is not a problem for God, who is by definition an eternally existent being, which is his problem. He's grown old, he wants to downsize, can't keep the place up but the universe keeps expanding, expanding, expanding. It's then, which is to say now, he envies his creatures, our natural talent for dying.

As I get older, what I fear isn't the loss of my life (while having an animal fear of dying) but the losses of my life – those defeats and dispossessions made irrevocable by death.

In time, my grief became largely disappointment that she died young and deserted me. I needed to see it as less a betrayal than a lesson: never love like that again.

I needed to get over my grief if I was to live and when I did – my life, a vital medium, seemed a slight thing, hardly worth maintaining if it could not bear the weight of her absence.

A kiss-off colliding with another kiss-off constitutes a kiss-on, or as the quantum behaviorists express it; -K + -K = K. It was delicious to suddenly understand that not only would the world go on happily without me (which is obvious) but that I would not go on (and here the discovery follows), happily without it.

He was content his life would tamp down to a residue of names, the places he had lived and people he had loved.

Microessays

History as genre is more tragic than literature. Literary characters lack the determinacy of bodily fate. Oedipus and Jocasta might end up as just another Updikean power couple. But the shell from Bismarck headed toward Hood doesn't deviate, ever. Yes, we can write "Hood survived her battle with Bismarck." And what is that – weak fiction. [10]

It's gonna be kinda sad, when China, unequivocally country number one, constantly touts the glories of Chinese culture and the Americans can make no reply except "baseball" and "the moon landing" because they've rejected "western civilization" as a prejudicial (and oppressive) promotion of a historically racist enterprise they self-righteously repudiate.

It is better to be an old aphorist (when one was once a young poet) than an old poet. (The aphorist sets out to articulate general truths that need not be beautiful or necessarily true, the poet to creation of verbal beauty. If the poet hasn't done that in the first forty years of his vocation (when words were lovers) it is unlikely he will later, when they are gummy chums. For best success, old aphorists should write poetically and old poets, aphoristically (as Eliot, in *Four Quartets*).[11]

Days are where our lives happen. Great defeats and victories wash into them like water in a ship's compartments, days contain and dilute them. Soon our days have an equal level, a standard style, even the hero and the mad have typical days and each is enriched by the resonance of all those that went before until weakened in our mind and senses, they (best case) lighten almost delightfully. That was our life – so many days.

We were well fortified and our lines were secure. There was no thought of giving up. Resistance had given us all the meaning anybody one would want. But suddenly there was a sense like a scent of spring – now we noticed, the enemy's wire was rusted, his flags, frivolous, tattered, the sentries were cardboard cut outs. The war had gone far from here, the world was busy with business, happy in its indifferent way. Now we were desperate for surrender, an elaborate formality that would recognized our struggle, not this sudden diminishment and daily desertion.

In a world of time and space and people, collisions are unavoidable. Some are of such a severe kind that time does not diminish them but is their medium; the collision goes on and on and one is never the same after because there is no after. Conventionally, one would want to live forever but the longer one lives the more likely one is to have a catastrophically continuous collision, the only repair of which is death. Your choice so to speak but only so to speak.

With advances in computing and bio-technology, the next phase of art will be in-brain consciousness, the artist using consciousness as his material, art experienced rather than as all visual art now is, observed. Of course, this is crass, as is all prognostication.

Style is not just the conveyer of thought but its substance. Commentary: the qualifying gesture, the whiff of irony (short, one hopes, of condescension), slaps of good humor and stabs at depth, these stylistic emanations reveal everything essential about my intellectual identity.

The self pitier is confident he can apply the application "a feeling sorry for" with greater attention to individual detail than any outside contriver – a true "do-it-yourselfer."

Against self-pity: keep in mind the world is large and every minute, second rather, a creature suffers an injury or injustice worse than your own. You need to set to work in the long line of minutes to come to prevent or sooth some creature's severer hurt. When in the rough reckoning of the universe, your own pain is highest ranked (and not by you), you will have earned the right to again dwell on it, with all the attendant satisfactions.

Increasingly, it seemed to him, in the face of so much culturally accumulated good art, the act of creation by non-talents was untrammeled assertion and presentation of ego. It was best to do nothing, a humility easy to take too much take pride in.[12]

How often one is hurt by the ordinary beauty of the world. The instruction of the hurt – that our egos are fragile and frivolous and yet selves are where we perceive and apprehend beauty. Our failure : we cannot love the world enough, we are wanting and this wanting to be and do better becomes the mainspring of our best creations (and sometimes, our worst actions).

Already, there's a gleam in our eyes and we're rubbing our hands in anticipation of the one foot increase (two, if we're lucky) in ocean levels set to inspire our heroic, beaver- determined labors: sea walls, pumping stations, mandatory migrations and new towns on the higher elevations. Meantime, except for the mini-archipelagoes of preservation (museums, libraries, historic houses and districts) the great dissolver inundates unabated: time's tide, always rising.[13]

Abruptly, in the midst of his recounting the latest emperor's judicial murders, Tacitus takes a time out to ponder the question "are our lives ruled by fate or by chance?" He has no answer. Mine is that 'chance' is simply one of the appearances of fate. Fate rules our lives in this universe, but in a quantum split generated multi-universe, fate here is merely one of infinite possibilities, *inevitability as chance*. It is a question we can get no purchase on; something is wrong with it similar to "why is there anything rather than nothing?" (when our empty concept of nothing only has meaning in a cosmos of something). Yet these questions engage us and they are safe ones compared to "why is the government corrupt" or "who owns what" or "how are these bad rulers made", inquiries that somewhere, in all eras, will get you killed, the fate of many of Tacitus's bold or loose lipped talkers. Tacitus himself survived, indeed prospered, a lean and hungry listener of the kind that tyrants, by fate or chance, sometimes overlook.

Nineteen Eighty-four. When O'Brien visits Winston Smith in his cell and Smith says "So they got you too." and O'Brien's replies, "they got me a long time ago", we experience the elation of recognition. In our capacity for complicity and betrayal, we too were gotten a long time ago.

All art is implemented by will, single mindedness and dedicated application. But these are methods easily acquired compared to what the artist must first acquire – a sense of the world's paradox and contradiction, an attentive adaptation to the environment of equivocation. The fabric of our lives, and hence of our art, is of a mingled and tangled yarn.

Reason and experience should prevent vanity since it is clear there is always somebody better at what you do than you, not to mention braver and more beautiful. This shouldn't encourage envy of known or putative "betters", since they are subject to the same physics – there is somebody better than they. While relative differences in skill are appraisable and real, *ultimately* value is distributive – we live not as points in hierarchies but as positions on networks.

American converts to Buddhism seem not to be aware (or care) that their adapted doctrines are tainted with the promotional and preservational biases of a class – the priests. Native devotees are alert to the enabling hypocrisies and make various doctrinal adjustments.

Schopenhauer avers that if you were to ask the dead if they wanted to live again, they'd say no. We know better. Ask them if would they like another sip of champagne, or another sunset seen. I haven't popped the big question; do they want to fuck again? Anybody left in the grave? Oh, that guy dying to have an encore performance as pessimistic poser.

What future societies (if there are any) will acutely criticize about our time is the lack of a philosophy or aesthetic of affect and our sad free-lance attempts to construct one from selective consumption. (Historically, the court societies of Japan, China and 18th France have come closest to living such a philosophy and for all their problems are worth our aspiration.)

After hundreds of miles of advance and months of battles, the panzer corps has conquered the city of the Volga. Too exhausted to advance and too weak to retreat, it's stuck in the rubble and surrounded. With the onset of winter, no reinforcements can get in; food and ammunition arrive in amounts insufficient to sustain even the depleted forces. It is courage, skill, and sacrifice that have placed the troops in this impossible position. If only they had failed earlier on. Hopes are fantastic: the Fuehrer will unleash a miracle weapon, the war will be won on another front. The temperature can't get any lower, guys to my left and right will die but somehow I will survive. An abstract of a specific horror, easily advanced as a general metaphor.[14]

Objectivity, events seek their truth value in interpretation – any action generates a myriad of interpretations. Subjectively, the succession of interpretations wants validation in an event, "what really happened". Put another way, historians operate along an axis of what/why, critics along why/what. This is to artificially diagram what is the continuous piston pulse of living, where all interpretations are events and every event is compounded with an interpretation (the most common being the one supplied by the automatic consciousness "this act requires no interpretation.") As Marx (Groucho) put it in his empathically matter-of-fact way, what's required is a sanity clause and two hard boiled eggs.

Three non-Botticelli portraits.

He had a superb visual sense, could fluently articulate new artistic forms verbally but all of his paintings were crude. He simply didn't have a practical artistic ability to implement his vision. This placed his friends in a dilemma. If they told him about his lack of talent, he'd either believe them and be hurt or not believing them, see it as an assault. So they said nothing; in his continued creative exertions he seemed both ludicrous and pathetic and therefore lovable. Lovable too for his effect on them, making them thus magnanimous.

While not clinically manic-depressive, she was very much a slash/burn and move-on type. Her job, her locale, a book she was reading, they were all fine until suddenly they weren't. With friends, she was more abiding but a similar physics was at work; she got a lot out of you and truth to tell she'd put a lot in. You were very valuable and then you weren't. After several cycles of cultivating and cropping, leached of resource, and dependent on her fertilizing inputs, you felt exhausted. You felt like dirt.

He was so brilliant he constantly generated and then under-
mined his intellectual positions, a one person Hegelian
thesis and antithesis without any stasis in synthesis. It was
all onrush of discourse and at such speed and fecundity
– he thought nothing notable about his thoughts – they
were incessantly successive and nothing worth sorting or
recording. Being around him was stressful not because of
his talk – which was at worst diverting and at best spell-
binding – but because his friends had to resist giving him
some injury, restraining the impulse to knock out some of
his brains right there so that he might amount to something.

The one young man in youth was cynical – a decade of
good luck makes him think better of himself and the
world generally. Another, starting out good tempered,
becomes after adverse events, skeptical and wary. Life,
like a steam hammer, has a way of pounding all of us
into similar tolerances.

Reviewing the Situation. No matter how intelligent you
are, the Situation is smarter and will baffle you. It is
always more durant; you may take temporary escape
in a book or film or sleep or a long walk but when
you are finished, it is always there like an Easter Island
head, looking at you with your own unaverting eyes.
It colonizes time, occupying the present, determining

your past in that every action was already pregnant and foreclosing the future since you can't imagine a prospect free of it; not a bore weight but a thing that makes you heavy, not a discrete hazard but an ingested pathology, not a blade thrust but a cancer. It compels endless negotiations over alternative realities (*not* futures), hinging on atom splits of "if only", "had I", "perhaps" – infinite iterations of "why" like starlings storm-thrown against the reactor's walls with no effect on its endless emissions, black radiation. That said, there are two or three good effects of the Situation. One may be propelled into art because the free creation of art, especially the generation of contradiction and limit (since the only true freedom is self-limitation: see Hegel) provides psychological relief and an alternative-affirmative compensatory "world". Death becomes an ally because only death has power to eliminate the Situation. And in dealing with a waitress, a cab driver, a nurse, an annoying co-worker, anyone, one's default approach may be one of polite consideration (nothing saintly), conceiving that as they go about their routines of living, smiling as required, they too are dealing with the Situation and really, you'd have to be downright mean to add to their burden. Not that that is a law of human interaction; victims are also, notoriously, victimizers – anything to avoid the endless free-fall of self-pity.

In his ignorance and arrogance, Trump is America (at its stupidest) so that even if you hated him in particular, you knew he or some other moron would be president someday, not as matter of complex causation but inevitably – as if you had gone back in time to strangle baby Hitler and come back to find that his worst substitute (some guy you never heard of) was not only still (2017) leader of a Greater Reich but the issuer of your time-traveled passport and all because it was destined by German political DNA. Moral: bad stuff is going to happen but it could always be worse. Maybe.

It was only in the first ten minutes of waking, after a long night of jostling dreams, as his mind strained to decipher a strange iterative bird-note, that he understood that his bright conscious life was the least of something jagged, immense and below the surface – moving.

Despite his extolling of life over art, it was plain even to him that his own life, with its underdeveloped or obvious characters and chaotic plot had less meaning than a $2.75 paperback romance novel. (And, while we're at it, a lot less romance if, come to think of it, embellished with more than one lurid cover).

In Aztec culture, only the nobles and priests on sacred occasions, under strict ritual rules, could drink alcohol and never to excess. The common people had to wait until they were sixty-five, at which time they could imbibe however much they wanted, day or night, at public expense – a brilliant bit of social engineering that combines Social Security, Medicare, elder hostelry, and carnival cruise in one toss.

Old men are funny. No matter how decrepit they feel, they can't see themselves in their mind's eye as any older than 39 or so (Jack Benny's jocular age). The codger in the wheel chair with an oxygen bottle envisions himself as a much younger man, one endowed with heroic, almost fetching handicaps. Every old geezer is looking forward, yes actually looking forward to the day, sure to sweeten his calendar, when he will meet the special nurse, caretaker, tax preparer that will perfectly partner his "May-December wedding."

Had Eve been murdered, Adam would have been the prime suspect – they did not bond around grief and were rancorous with recriminations – at l least until little Cain came along. But several thousand marriages later, in a much more multitudinous world, what does it say about mankind that if a wife is killed, it is always the husband who must first be cleared by alibi, location, or forensics before the investigation can proceed? With murdered husbands, it is more complex since any man worth his salt should have made at least one enemy other than his wife – if she is one and usually she isn't.

Let me get back to you about that. It seems the deer will eat any plant except the coniferous and thorny. My garden has its defenses – chicken wire and stakes, human hair and urine – that are half effective. I've had my losses. I sometimes see them in the grey light of dawn or twilight, their motion – movement and stillness, wary and almost, I think, arrogant. They are beautiful and who would deny beauty the right of trespass?

One of the delights of ageing, the extraordinary bouquet of self-off-gassing aromas: burnt motor, hot metal, old flowers, makes me pity youth's clean impoverishment.

Entire eras, peopled with individuals, act solely in the present tense, with no cognition of history, its complex causations and continuous consequences. Humans are, to that extent, like animals, although incapacitated from ignorance rather than natural innocence. As long as we fail to act as fully aware historical agents, we will continue to do what we are good at, making, contra Hegel, a mess of history.

If you consider his conception of *Geist*, its self-alienation and contradiction, its embodiment in things and minds, its vast branching out via thesis and antithesis into the absolute of everything that is, it's clear Hegel was a kind of quasi kabbalist even if it is hard to say how consciously he was or how direct the Jewish influence. I'm surely not the only person to think this (if true, the idea is accessible) but it is nonetheless original with me. It took me years to get there but it's the kind of journey where time in transit is irrelevant. What matters is arrival.

It is always a good idea to name drop Kant, Hegel, Nietzsche, Derrida, Foucault, Lacan into your discourse or book. Two or three people out of a hundred, your appreciators, might admire your acquaintanceship with such savants. Only one out of a thousand will know enough to know if you know what you are talking about. The odds are in your favor. (It's rather touching, the old, old story; we trust people to trust.) And it's brave too, even at the advantageous odds, even if you're only being bogus or boastful. As _____ said, "Contradiction is the engine of truth."[15]

Brush strokes made by a long-stilled hand, words and notes actually or mentally voiced by a death dissolved throat, all art is memento mori. Even contemporary art, with the creator standing right beside it, has passed beyond the rim of the living and become sepulchral. It's easy to understand why most people, cheerful – busy with business of the world types – have no traffic with such morbidity.

Hegel, Herder, Husserl, Heidegger, Horkheimer – just to name the h's – all that philosophical lavation, what did it all amount to? Hogwash. What was needed? The computer I hold in my hand, cozy as a chipmunk. I am always connected, never alone; always busy, never bored. My simian brain is lit-up, delighted. When we were "'deep" we were never happy, nor meant to be — deep, that is. Any critic who would say our contentment is shallow misses the point: our shallowness is deep and our fulfillment found not as masters of the universe but as multitaskers of the cyberverse. Geist was nothing, gizmo's the thing. (Here a footnote to a footnote might be nice: Geist in Hegelian philosophy denotes the capacity of the human mind, individually and socially, and its *progressive* manifestations in art, history and ideas.) [16]

Arthurian. The sword Excalibur and The Grail are (obviously) potent symbols of the male and female "principles". They never meet in union except as a field of force where mere men and women make (in the sense of both production and repair) the messy bed of history. *Comealot*

I had decided to relay the old flag stone path, overgrown with grass. I probed the sod with a pick ax and when I got a tap, moved the point forward until I reached the stone's edge, hooking the point and levering to unearth the rock. Suddenly I realized: I had pulled the stone from the sward and my mind began to riff, theme and variations. Arthur had done the same deed, reversed, pulling the sword from the stone to win the crown and Guinevere. With Second Prize, had there been one, being the crown and two Guineveres.

Note: *Two Guineveres.* An adulterated coin of the Arthurian era, having two faces (technically, the coin lacked an obverse) with heads of Guinevere. Popularly, the coin was known as a "Twin Guin","Guin" becoming the common term for money as something that passes from man to man yet doesn't lose value. None of this is meant to disparage Guinevere. She was, in the words of an old song, "a whole lot of woman who needed a whole lot of man"(or a pound with a Euro). Arthur, for all kinds of good reasons (iodine deficiency, burdens of state and excessively good manners), was a bit of a sad sack, in bed and out. Lancelot, on the other hand, wasn't called Lancelot for nothing. All such cases should be viewed – especially if there is no malice involved and perhaps even if there is provided the malice isn't deadly – with equanimity, given the human condition, the incongruity of what we call spirit being embodied in what we know is flesh. *Definition:* Excalibur; 1. Arthur's sword. 2. Any large or oversized weapon, an **X-caliber**. *"Ronnie who had only seen guns in movies and as accoutrements to cops suddenly needed one. The pawn shop was a dust collector located between a shoe store flogging the latest decades old V-J Day models and a perpetually going out of business haberdashery. Entering, startled by the open-close sign banging behind him, he couldn't process the place, all kinds of stuff all over, overlooked, high up on the three walls he could see, by mounted animal heads – a tiger, various disappointed bucks and a bear over the counter who had glared in better days. The proprietor, who looked like somebody's substitute uncle, was polishing something that could have been anything. Ronnie was only in medias res in his aria of throat clearing when Unc looked up. "You got any **x-calibers**?" Ronnie asked flatly, like it was a statement. As the old man turned away, it was easy to mistake his condescending grin for fraternal feeling and technical recognition. Meantime the bear, closer, seemed friendlier with decrepitude, sporting yellow teeth and dusty eyes that wouldn't have minded a brushing."* From *The Hollow Point*, by Ray Chandler.

This is the way my mind works, set-off, going in a circle, wagging its tail, occasionally barking at a tree. If I could present nothing without the expression of a certain quality, I yet spare you the excessiveness of the quantity.

Poetry, etc.

Having read so many published poems worse than mine own, I finally sickened of the entire genre, which made a kind of clearance for a potential better poetry since none of mine would ever again be printed (For bibliographical purposes, it should be recorded that my final composed poem, *Umbrage*, was published in Pamplemousse, vol. 4, no.2, 2017. Appreciators of my prior poetry will detect tonalities indicative of a new departure, leading nowhere.)

Explicit memory;

those dying phlox bruised by moonlight and wind

a certified neurological entity,

as if to braise from portal and window an illumination: later

my mainline to pain, a cry's quick ululation.

Thank you again for the infusion

declining the shape of species and fields away

summer's dew jewels, crystals on the rose lips

the wet light focused into liquid yearning

forgiveness, something done for oneself, ungenerous.

Allow me to proceed, altruistically, to revenge,

a project not yet yet finished.

And if I live aslant and in darkness,

well, it is a place of definite delineation

when the alternative, our noon tide of sun,

was a wash, nothing, a needle wanting shadow.

Poetry is never there (here), immediate in full dimensionality; it requires considerable mediation, conduction by consciousness through time so that every word has to deserve and overcome the inertia of this labor which is why it is harder to write a good poem than paint a good painting and why there is so much more bad poetry than good art when there is no lack of good art. (In a poem, every word resonates with every other, dead words are more than particularly damaging, they void whole networks of interchange. In painting, you can always smudge a blot and the greatest masters have.)

Here is a common bromide: one becomes a writer by writing every day. Well, one becomes a pisser, pissing every day. The relevant question is not the frequency but the product: water or wine. A crude conclusion but no more than the inciting proposition.

I lack any talent for it but enjoy painting, the coordination of hand/eye and conceptualization entrances me and I lose all sense of self. As a poet, with some aptitude for it, the same sense of focus only occurred about ten times when, in my forties, I did my best work. The difference is: I poured myself (out of myself) into painting; the poems poured themselves into me. The result was the same but as any artist will appreciate, it is a sameness with a difference.

I told the students that wanting to be a poet was not enough, one needed to be one. No point in confusing the issue with those that needed to want to be one.

Poetry is intensified language. That's it – but there is a lot to it.

The ideal aphorism springs fully formed from the head of its creator, like Athena from Zeus. The aphorism that requires composition to be finished is immediately exposed, via its inchoateness, to a pathology of possibilities, literature itself, and emerges, if it does, deformed by the battle to survive, stumbling, stammering, and always too long.

The truth telling tone of the aphorism annoys/fatigues as quickly as one pure note repeated on the piano; one yearns for the extended and structured distractions of a sonata even if, in any of its instantiations, that was what drove one for relief to the singleton sounding.[17]

It's a shame American poetry is debased (as flat, undistinguished and as ugly as Queens, New York) because it is the laboratory for the invention and refurbishment of language. If it is asserted that language does this naturally, keep in mind that such renewal is always the work of some individual, working unconsciously and serendipitously as a poet.

Three times in two weeks reviewers have praised the famous poet for "her small body of work, only a hundred poems." Fifty too many, surely. [Granted mediocre poems may be useful as kindling or scaffolding for better. Having fulfilled that function, they should be gotten rid of. Any poet should relish the right to selectively eradicate his work. Now, with most poetry deposited on web sites, it is technically possible to obliterate, with the touch of cursor and button, every trace of dross verbiage. My publishers at Winston-Smith were the first to offer this essential service.]

Anselm Hollo, whom I respect as a rebel poet and faithful translator, writes that the practitioners of the "New Poetics" were in essential revolt against the pomposities, ironies and refined (when they were) whines of the dominant mainstream style. A good project, in theory. But nothing is more instantly staid than the self-indulgent obscurantist pompositeurs of the LANGUAGE type or more tiresome than the wink-wink antics of their bemedaled, just off to the side clown, the utterly authorized antic (*Library of America,* in his lifetime!) Ashbury.

When X, the distinguished critic informs you in the promotion of his latest fave poet that he, Y, has written twenty-two books of poetry, X (the critic) is providing valuable instruction. You now know that Y is definitely ignorable. Likewise, when you are informed that "B" only wrote 100 poems, you know she is worth inspecting and indeed, only ninety of them are utterly mediocre. (Nothing demonstrates the ineptitude (or is that *politics)* of American critical evaluation than the elevation of this polite, *entirely harmless,* versifier to the status of major poet.)

It's true, I have no patience for aesthetic mediocrity. The cultural establishment (composed of professors, publishers and poets) that facilitates our acclimation, as readers and writers, to mediocrity is a destructive dynamo that works against the creation of quality poems or their recognition should they miraculously appear. And who am I to say so – a practitioner who, in a life time of half-hearted commitment, has written one or two beautiful lines.[18]

Writing is as much a matter of cultivation as composition. So many books are spoiled either by too soon a harvesting – which results in a lack of savor – or by a lingering that leaves them rotten (or at least lifeless) with overdevelopment. For learning art, a garden is a better situation than a classroom which is why I have always encouraged my students to branch out, eschewing the MFA in favor of a degree in horticulture or agriculture, fields where culture is an essential, vital and deeply instructive element.

It is much easier to write a poem than write a good one which is why, in every era, the state of poetry is deplorable though these days (2017) from the effect of larger demographics and a more democratic literary culture, there is more bad poetry more highly praised than ever. To be accredited in such an environment, even Shakespeare must be shown to have been a bad poet, which explains the forty year crusade of American Shakespeare scholar Gary Taylor to establish the jejune little lyric "Shall I die" as Shakespeare's work. I am not being dyspeptic since none of this matters. The prominent critic and poetry promoter David Orr has himself said that contemporary American poetry is a minor hobby (like collecting porcelain figurines), a taste (like beer flavored with elderberries), a boutique bar with dubious food and unreliable service. It matters so much less than the spectacular exertions of NASCAR, which every weekend involves a hundred thousand appreciators and millions of dollars. The poor state of poetry should only concern us when poetry, in reaction, is again a vital cultural force that has initiated if not yet concluded the immune response that identifies and expels dreck.[19] How many novels have I read and stayed with in the expectation that they would improve and sometimes they did. With poetry, one is immediately immersed in a field of force, strong or weak. Any subsequent alterations in the charge are minute.

Browsing the PR (British) and PS (American) call numbered stacks at the university library, one notices more slim volumes in the former than in the latter. Many of them are contemporary plays, testifying to the vigor of British theatre, which in turn contributes significantly to the quality of British poetry. Any young poet has the opportunity to see that on stage the success of a scene, a play, an entire company, may hinge on one word. The verbal tolerances are narrow and the environment dangerous (people leaving at the interval). A lesson is presented: every word matters. Lacking this tuition, American poetry is lackadaisical, self-indulgent and complacent especially when it goes through the motions of being radical and nothing, absolutely nothing is at stake. There is no present, operational danger, no sense that configuring of words, as when an actor articulates on stage, is exacting, vital and hazardous. Poetry cannot replicate the stage's risk but the poet should emulate it in his awareness that his art is hard, that talent is rare and must be cultivated, that the prevailing aesthetic slope favors the mediocre, that no one (especially his fellow poets) wants him to succeed, that external rewards are unlikely (and essentially meaningless), that this awareness is a crucially advantaging adaptation without which his poems are almost certain to be comfortably enfolded into the herds of dead words, just another bum steer.

I enjoyed crafting "aphorisms" which blended the economy and allusiveness of poetry with the discursiveness and declarativity of philosophy. But I came to understand that their only significance (including the classic formulations of Rochefoucauld and Chamfort) was auto-biographical, what had been meaningful, maybe, to one man once. And what did that mean?

Writers write for many reasons – from excess verbal energy, from ambition, from need to tell a tale or make a point. Mine was the practice of a dark art from a dark place, nothing allied with death of destruction but without any co-efficient either in positivity, purpose or position. It was like sex, not willed but affirmed, private but revealing, personal and impersonal, nasty and nice and vice versa. My writing had an aspiration to art and art requires a public dimension. Exposed there (this book and the others), I felt like pornographer, his moderate reservations overcome too easily and a long time ago, his pleasure slight and slightly sick, his best intention – a provocation, the X-rated, "art film" director pointing with seeming indifference to his actors – words, words, words, fucking.

Notes

1   Johnson predicted our antic attention spans but not the long grey procession of processed words—this fortnight's latest four-hundred-page novel versus a fortune cookie's scroll of focus. The battle of carnival and Lent, now better than ever. This state of stalemate will be short-lived. It should be obvious to any interested observer that visual art's future lies in various inversions of VR, literature's in complex narrative and multi-media programming, a form of "gaming". The two strains will unite to make the "complete work" of art, around 2030.

2   The aphorist feels truth, given the multiverse of existing subsumptive systems, is best expressed anti-systematically. Buddhism, Hegelianism, the Kabbalah are all false in their aspect of totalization. Even physics … Minerva's magpie is wiser than her owl.

3   This is from the position of the creator. For the consumer, certain instances of art are themselves wounds, i.e. tragedy. *Othello* is the definitive English example. The play that is usually said to be such, *King Lear,* isn't, being a war horse that any serious director, seasoned actor and established company can turn into a panto horse, its iconic scenes: Tom without an overcoat, Lear without an umbrella, Gloucester stumbling blind to Dover, Cordelia

as cord wood – played, in a sense, for laughs, our canned emotive guffaws. Sufficiently refurbished as *Weird Lear,* the king a man of thirty, his daughters 13-14-15 (intense adolescents), Gloucester robbed not (just) of his eyes but his cock and balls, the play might yet transport us to "the tragic", a place beyond tears -- the numbness of total vulnerability. If these means seem sensational, and they are, so are all immune responses (in this case, against theatrical tedium).

4   This said, looking out a window, thinking on time and space, observing thoughts arise and dissipate (including the conceits of self), the lowest level of vipassana, won't get you very far. However, there is no proof that going further along these lines is anything other than a typically human exercise in excessance.

5   Schopenhauer refers to "the labyrinth of life that we navigate by error". He is ever the wittiest of the jestful Germans, though I prefer Hegel with his long face, slow delivery and stumble-bum manner. Check out that historic video on YouTube of his opening routine at the Absolut (Vodka) Lounge (Berlin, 1836). He shambles out to the spotlight, already down a few flagons of Rhenish and says "So I got up this morning (comma) and Geist (pronounced close to "guess") what happened?" The original Droopy Dog, he peers out with watery eyes and bad haircut, the look of long suffering. An extended pause drags snickers from the audience. He repeats "So I got up this morning

and Geist" (pronounced correctly this time and with a verbally signaled dash) – what happened." Groans and moans! I was finding Heidegger fun too, with his rat's stare, Hitler-wanna-be mustache, nattering monologues on "Being" punctuated by falsetto renderings of *The Sound of Music* ("climb every mountain, ford every stream ..."), until I noticed the NSDAP button glinting on one suspender of his lederhosen.

6   This is not to criticize Ruskin's over-valuation of art when his criticism is, in its entirely, one of the highest instantiations of (verbal) art and hence not to be judged strictly on the stance of its propositional postures.

7   The large white rabbit, with a distinct leporine resemblance to Henry James, who made these pronouncements, bolted down his bunny hole before I could counter with "if too much pornography hasn't killed sex – and it hasn't, why should we credit any of your negations?"

8   This statement was awarded (2006) the bronze medal in the Modern Language Association's annual Dicta-Dicta-Dicta Competition. Along with the gong, the award consisted of a five day, "all expenses paid" stay at the Venice Hotel and Casino, Las Vegas, featuring performances in the Rialto Room by such top-drawer groups as Rus Kind and The Seven Lamps.

9   An aphorism of the classical sort, overdosed at the rate of one-a-day. See Rambeau, Sylvestris. *Auf der Aphorismus: seine Bedeutung und Anwendung als eine immanente System der Unvollstandigkeit* (Berlin, 1889)

10   This simplifies something very complex. Historians, like novelists, work with characters, situations, settings. The difference is that history is a matter of discovery or uncovering while fiction is one of development, which is harder and most writers aren't up to it. Since a writer spends only a few months dedicated to what any human spends a life time on – the development of a character – historical personages are generally richer than fictional ones. I concur with the view of the estimable scholar, Inga Clendinnen, "I am persuaded that we listen differently to stories which are "real", however naively or awkwardly reported, from stories however beguiling, which we know to be invented. With a work of fiction, we marvel at the fictioneer's imagination. With real thought and actions presented for our scrutiny we are brought to wonder at ourselves." But let's give the last word here to the novelist Robert Stone. "Never allow facts to get in the way of truth."

11   A young poet is a paragon; a young aphorist, an oxymoron.

12   Shakespeare is emphatic: it is better for a poet to write nothing than write inferior verse "impairing beauty." (Sonnet 83)

13   Or put another way – as deeply indoctrinated economic "factors", we unconsciously-conscientiously accept climate change as the cost of doing business and a golden opportunity – the planet, teeming with populational and informational prospects, one hot property.

14   The case can be made that boys who grew up under the post-1933 Nazi education system and who as young men were drafted into the German war machine were also victims of fascism, however, the ethical situation is complex. "To his officers, the common soldier was expendable the moment he ceased to fulfil his functions; to the defeated population, he was the embodiment of the *Herrenrasse*, standing above the law, deciding about death and life according to the dictates of his whim." (See Omer Bartov's *Hitler's Army: soldiers, Nazis, and war in the Third Reich*, Oxford, 1991) Over 100,000 German soldiers were captured at Stalingrad. 90% of those below the rank of major (over 95% of the prisoners) died while 90% of those ranked major and higher survived ten years captivity to return to their homes. So much for Stalinistic regard for the proletariat.

15   Though explanations are onerous, it should be said that this passage is not meant as braggartry or connivance but as humour in the spirit of Hegel (see *On Sense-Certainty,* Baillie (trans.) 1931 ed., p. 159.

16   Heidegger writes (in *schwarze Heft 2*) "Only with increasing depth goes genuine breath expand." (Rojcewicz, trans). He is responding to Publius Porcius, a second-century (AD) student of Lucretius, who wrote (in *De Re Barbecuria*) "Only with increasing shallowness does genuine depth deepen.' Both statements are hogwash. But if you must wash a hog – not something I 'd ever recommend – it's best to do it whole hog and use quality hogwash, such as Heidegger's "Old Boar" brand. [However despicable, Heidegger gets credit for seriously grappling with the question "how can we live authentically?" After the diversionary decades of sex, family and career, the question again presents itself with greater clarity, if with less intensity than when it first did, in adolescence. Something about us looks at ourselves and the world and asks "what should I be doing?" The answer will be different for each individual but elements of the solution must surely involve the creation of art (or the practice of an art), the protection of what is true and beautiful and the alleviation of human and animal misery. Okay, this is my soapbox, I bought it and I'm standing on it, the soap used up a long time ago in the sex baths. And yes, of course, the answer we're looking for was no doubt those dedicated decades of sex and family and work that slipped away which now I recall as spans of application, periods of reflection, spells of sound and fury, all of it

signifying something but not I think the authentication of life more than the scope of this present. ("In the case of life, all of Thinking's thought tires out, the omnipresence of the simple in the manifold of the external presents for reflection an absolute contradiction and incomprehensible mystery." (Hegel, the "*Jena Logic*", Nelson trans.)

17   As stated, this proposition articulates a dated binary opposition between a single note sounding and a multi-note composition. By 2017, numerous "one note" compositions exists, such as Randy Gibson's *The Four Pillars Appearing from the Equal D...* , a three hour work based on iterations of the seven Ds of the piano keyboard that sounds far better than its title (which continues for twelve more words), if of less interest than West Wind's popular pieces for chimes, none of which can compared to the extraordinary work of Nora Felis (who also performs under the name "Nora the Cat"), the most revered and renowned and justly so of minimalist classical composers. I should note that Nora, whose music, easily retrievable on the web, I much enjoy, is distantly related to my companion Rosaline Felis but we have never met her.

18   It may be asserted that I have uncritically promoted my paintings but as they are deployed for the very limited purpose of providing visual stimulation (illustration) and in hope that they will be improved by association with the text, such placement condones rather than confutes my sense of their mediocrity.

19   Cleanth Brooks writes "In giving up our criteria of good and bad, we have, as a consequence begun to give up our concept of poetry as well". Granted, this is a judgment, based on a lengthy series of other judgments; there is no grounding out of the gyre of argument. That said, good art generates a sophisticated series of critical judgments, mimetic to the actual and potential effects of the art object itself. This gauge is not infallible; there are fads in criticism and emperor's new clothes enthusiasms and what becomes the focus of interest is often the result of sheer accident. But it is the best objective gauge we have. Intuition, alone, is not to be trusted. [Watching the Lipizzaners dance, I have moved to tears in the conviction that I am witnessing the greatest cultural achievement of mankind. And just an inch of Scotch (MacTesco's) renders Rockwell greater than Rembrandt. There are, no doubt, even more deplorable examples.]

The Author

was born in Norfolk, Virginia and sometimes attended the University of Virginia. He has written several books. His poetry and critical essays have appeared in various publications, here and there. In 2013, he retired as Senior Cataloger at Harvard University's Graduate School of Design and returned to Charlottesville where he tends a garden and minds the cat. At the time of this writing, he is still alive.

The Author